Your F

I wanted to show my appreciatio... ... ... e put together a free gift for you.

Slowcooker Essentials Cookbook

http://thezenfactory.com/nutri_ninja_pro_free_book/

Just visit the link above to download it now.

I know you will love this gift.

Thanks!

Table of Content

Introduction	8
Healthy Coconut Orange Smoothie	9
Ingredients:	9
Directions:	9
Antioxidant Creamy Strawberries Smoothie	10
Ingredients:	10
Directions:	10
Glowing Skin Green Banana Smoothie	11
Ingredients:	11
Directions:	11
Liver Detox Strawberry Green Tea Smoothie	12
Ingredients:	12
Directions:	12
Energy Fuel Creamy Banana Dates Smoothie	14
Ingredients:	14
Directions:	14
Vitamin C Booster Lemon Apple Smoothie	15
Ingredients:	15
Directions:	15
ORAC Blueberry Mint Smoothie	17
Ingredients:	17
Directions:	17
Weight Loss Creamy Peach Smoothie	19
Ingredients:	19
Directions:	19
Great Digestion Green Pineapple Smoothie	20
Ingredients:	20

Directions: 20
Clean Tropical Pineapple Mango Smoothie 21
    Ingredients: 21
    Directions: 21
Live Enzyme Golden Papaya Carrot Smoothie 22
    Ingredients: 22
    Directions: 22
High Fiber Banana Almond Smoothie 24
    Ingredients: 24
    Directions: 24
Anti-Aging Avocado Smoothie 25
    Ingredients: 25
    Directions: 25
SupergoodSpring Almond Punch 26
    Ingredients: 26
    Directions: 26
Bones Strengthening Cashews Smoothie 27
    Ingredients: 27
    Directions: 27
Healthy Gut Creamy Apple Prunes Smoothie 28
    Ingredients: 28
    Directions: 28
Kid-Friendly Cinnamony Prune Smoothie 30
    Ingredients: 30
    Directions: 30
Iodine Booster Green Algae Powder 32
    Ingredients: 32
    Directions: 32

Detox Pear Cucumber Smoothie	33
Ingredients:	33
Directions:	33
Iron Booster Beet Apple Smoothie	35
Ingredients:	35
Directions:	35
Antioxidant Rich Minty Berries Apple Smoothie	36
Ingredients:	36
Directions:	36
Cleansing Bluish Ginger Smoothie	37
Ingredients:	37
Directions:	37
Detox Lemon Smoothie	38
Ingredients:	38
Directions:	38
Alkalizing Cranberry Smoothie	39
Ingredients:	39
Directions:	39
Radiant Skin Cherry Berry Smoothie	41
Ingredients:	41
Directions:	41
Anti-Aging Bomb Berries Summit	43
Ingredients:	43
Directions:	43
Healthy Heart Pear Avocado Smoothie	44
Ingredients:	44
Directions:	44
Super Models Secret Creamy Goji Berries Smoothie	45

Ingredients: 45

Directions: 45

Green Monster Jicama Smoothie 46

Ingredients: 46

Directions: 46

Alkalizing Orange Smoothie 47

Ingredients: 47

Directions: 47

Healthy Liver Limy Coconut Smoothie 48

Ingredients: 48

Directions: 48

Clean Gut Spicy Tomato Smoothie 50

Ingredients: 50

Directions: 50

Superfood Creamy Spirulina Smoothie 51

Ingredients: 51

Directions: 51

Cleansing Mango Kale Smoothie 52

Ingredients: 52

Directions: 52

Glowing Skin Summery Strawberry Lemon Smoothie 53

Ingredients: 53

Directions: 53

Fat Burner Lemony Apple Smoothie 54

Ingredients: 54

Directions: 54

Fight Cholesterol Lime Almond Smoothie 55

Ingredients: 55

Directions:	55
Kid-Friendly Tropical Avocado Smoothie	56
Ingredients:	56
Directions:	56
Clear Skin Pear Summer Smoothie	58
Ingredients:	58
Directions:	58
Blood Pressure Cucumber Beet Smoothie	59
Ingredients:	59
Directions:	59
Red Velvet Veggies Smoothie	60
Ingredients:	60
Directions:	60
Forever Young Blue Royal Smoothie	61
Ingredients:	61
Directions:	61
Weight Loss Almond Berry Smoothie	62
Ingredients:	62
Directions:	62
Perfect Morning Green Spring Smoothie	63
Ingredients:	63
Directions:	63
Healthy Dessert Vanilla Caramel	64
Ingredients:	64
Directions:	64
No Constipation Cheesy Vanilla Tart	65
Ingredients:	65
Directions:	65

Huge Muscle Protein Berry Smoothie	66
Ingredients:	66
Directions:	66
Post Workout Creamy Honey Tofu	67
Ingredients:	67
Directions:	67
Energy Booster Banana Coffee	68
Ingredients:	68
Directions:	68
Glowing Green Kale Smoothie	69
Ingredients:	69
Directions:	69
Conclusion	71

Introduction

Nutri Ninja Master blender have been and still one of the best blenders ever, you can blend in it anything such as nuts, ice, veggies, fruits... and they will literary come out so smooth and creamy. When it comes to this miracle blender, I like to use it for making my own smoothies!!

Throw on a bunch of healthy ingredients that includes nuts, fruits and veggies by following one of the recipes below then let your master blender to do all the work for you.

Welcome to the ultimate guide of the best smoothies your taste buds will ever taste, whether you are vegan, paleo or you don't follow any diet, there are plenty of recipes that will suit your taste and load your body with energy so that you can ran you errands and go through your day without feeling exhausted as you are used to!!

After getting used to drink at least 1 cup of your favorite smoothie a day, you will gradually notice how your life and body will improve. You will become healthier and burn lot of fat in a record time not to mention that you will also strengthen your immunity system and protect yourself from many fatal diseases!!

For teens and adults, these smoothies are perfect for everybody because they are simply natural and you can never go wrong with what is natural!!!

Healthy Coconut Orange Smoothie
(ready in about 2 minutes | Servings 2)

Ingredients:

- 1 ½ orange, peeled and sliced
- 2 tablespoons of flaxseeds
- 2 ½ cups of coconut water
- 2 kiwis, peeled and sliced

Directions:

1. Combine all the ingredients in your Ninja Blender and blend them on high speed for 45 sec.
2. Once the time is up, serve it right away and enjoy.

Antioxidant Creamy Strawberries Smoothie
(ready in about 2 minutes | Servings 2)

Ingredients:

- 1 cup of ice cubes
- ¾ cup of blueberries
- ½ cup of strawberries
- 2 teaspoons of ground flax seeds

Directions:

1. Combine all the ingredients in your Ninja Blender and blend them on high speed for 30 to 45 sec.
2. Once the time is up, serve it right away and enjoy.

Glowing Skin Green Banana Smoothie
(ready in about 2 minutes | Servings 2)

Ingredients:

- 1 ½ cups of spinach
- ¼ cup of lemon juice
- 2 ½ cups of soy milk
- 1 ½ bananas
- 2 tablespoons of sunflower seeds
- ¼ cup of avocado
- 3 tablespoons of sweetener

Directions:

1. Combine all the ingredients in your Ninja Blender and blend them on high speed for 45 sec.
2. Once the time is up, serve it right away and enjoy.

Liver Detox Strawberry Green Tea Smoothie

(ready in about 2 minutes | Servings 2)

Ingredients:

- 3 cups of strawberries
- 2 tablespoons of sweetener
- 2 cups of coconut water
- 2 tablespoons of green tea powder
- 1 ½ banana
- ¼ cup of plain yogurt
- 3 tablespoons of chia seeds

Directions:

1. Combine all the ingredients in your Ninja Blender and blend them on high speed until they become smooth and creamy.
2. Serve your smoothie right away and enjoy.

Energy Fuel Creamy Banana Dates Smoothie
(ready in about 2 minutes | Servings 2)

Ingredients:

- 1 cup of milk
- ¼ cup of dates, pitted
- 1 banana
- 1 cup of kale leaves
- 1 cup of arugula

Directions:

1. Combine all the ingredients in your Ninja Blender and blend them on high speed for 30 to 45 sec.
2. Once the time is up, serve it right away and enjoy.

Vitamin C Booster Lemon Apple Smoothie
(ready in about 2 minutes | Servings 2)

Ingredients:

- 2 ½ cups of coconut water
- 1 ½ apples
- ¼ of lemon juice
- 2 cups of kale leaves
- 2 carrots, finely chopped

Directions:

1. Combine all the ingredients in your Ninja Blender and blend them on high speed for 1 min.

2. Once the time is up, serve it right away and enjoy.

ORAC Blueberry Mint Smoothie
(ready in about 2 minutes | Servings 2)

Ingredients:

- 1 ½ cup of strawberries
- 2 ½ cups of coconut water
- 1 ½ cups of blueberries
- ¼ cup of mint leaves
- 2 tablespoon of lemon juice
- 2 teaspoon of chia seeds

Directions:

1. Combine all the ingredients in your Ninja Blender and blend them on high speed for 45 sec.
2. Once the time is up, serve it right away and enjoy.

Weight Loss Creamy Peach Smoothie
(ready in about 2 minutes | Servings 2)

Ingredients:

- 2 cups of peaches, sliced
- 2 cups of milk
- 1 cup of blueberries

Directions:

1. Combine all the ingredients in your Ninja Blender and blend them on high speed for 30 sec.
2. Once the time is up, serve it right away and enjoy.

Great Digestion Green Pineapple Smoothie
(ready in about 2 minutes | Servings 2)

Ingredients:

- 2 tablespoons of chia seeds
- 2 cups of coconut water
- 1 ½ cups of kale, finely chopped
- 1 ½ cups of mango, finely chopped
- 2 cups of pineapple chunks

Directions:

1. Combine all the ingredients in your Ninja Blender and blend them on high speed for 35 sec.
2. Once the time is up, serve it right away and enjoy.

Clean Tropical Pineapple Mango Smoothie
(ready in about 2 minutes | Servings 2)

Ingredients:

- 2 tablespoons of chia seeds
- 1 ½ cups of pineapple chunks
- 2 ½ cups of coconut water
- 1 cup of mango chunks

Directions:

1. Combine all the ingredients in your Ninja Blender and blend them on high speed for 50 sec.
2. Once the time is up, serve it right away and enjoy.

Live Enzyme Golden Papaya Carrot Smoothie
(ready in about 2 minutes | Servings 2)

Ingredients:

- 1 teaspoon of fresh ginger, peeled and sliced
- ½ cup of ice cubes
- 1 orange, sliced
- ½ cup of pear juice
- ½ carrot, sliced
- ½ papaya, sliced

Directions:

1. Combine all the ingredients in your Ninja Blender and blend them on high speed for 45 sec.
2. Once the time is up, serve it right away and enjoy.

High Fiber Banana Almond Smoothie
(ready in about 2 minutes | Servings 2)

Ingredients:

- 1 ½ banana
- 2 ½ cups of coconut water
- ¾ cup of almonds
- ¾ cup of dry oatmeal
- 2 tablespoons of honey

Directions:

1. Combine all the ingredients in your Ninja Blender and blend them on high speed for 45 sec.
2. Once the time is up, serve it right away and enjoy.

Anti-Aging Avocado Smoothie
(ready in about 2 minutes | Servings 2)

Ingredients:

- 2 cups of blueberries
- 2 tablespoons of flaxseed
- 2 avocados
- 2 tablespoons of honey
- 2 ½ cups of coconut water

Directions:
1. Combine all the ingredients in your Ninja Blender and blend them on high speed for 40 sec.
2. Once the time is up, serve it right away and enjoy.

SupergoodSpring Almond Punch
(ready in about 2 minutes | Servings 2)

Ingredients:

- 1 cup of kale
- 2 tablespoons of wheat bran
- 10 almonds
- 1 ½ cups of almond milk
- ½ avocado
- ½ cup of broccoli

Directions:

1. Combine all the ingredients in your Ninja Blender and blend them on high speed for 30 to 45 sec.
2. Once the time is up, serve it right away and enjoy.

Bones Strengthening Cashews Smoothie
(ready in about 2 minutes | Servings 2)

Ingredients:

- 15 cashews
- 1 ½ cups of almond milk
- ½ banana
- ½ cup of blueberries
- 4 tablespoons of wheat bran
- 1 cup of kale

Directions:

1. Combine all the ingredients in your Ninja Blender and blend them on high speed for 45 sec.
2. Once the time is up, serve it right away and enjoy.

Healthy Gut Creamy Apple Prunes Smoothie
(ready in about 2 minutes | Servings 2)

Ingredients:

- 6 prunes, pitted
- ½ banana
- ½ cup of plain yogurt
- ½ cup of apple sauce
- 1 tablespoon of Epsom Salt
- ½ cup of spring water
- ½ cup of ice cubes

Directions:

1. Combine all the ingredients in your Ninja Blender and blend them on high speed for 45 sec.

2. Once the time is up, serve it right away and enjoy.

Kid-Friendly Cinnamony Prune Smoothie
(ready in about 2 minutes | Servings 2)

Ingredients:

- 1 cup of ice cubes
- 5 prunes, pitted
- 1 cup of apple juice
- ½ teaspoon of cinnamon powder
- 2 tablespoon of honey
- 1 cup of plain yogurt

Directions:

1. Combine all the ingredients in your Ninja Blender and blend them on high speed for until they become smooth.

2. Serve your smoothie right away and enjoy.

Iodine Booster Green Algae Powder
(ready in about 2 minutes | Servings 2)

Ingredients:

- ½ cup of parsley leaves
- ½ cup of cilantro leaves
- ½ cup of spinach, finely chopped
- 2 apples, finely chopped
- 4 kale leaves
- 2 tablespoons of blue green algae powder
- 2 ½ cups of coconut water
- ½ ginger root, peeled and sliced

Directions:

1. Combine all the ingredients in your Ninja Blender and blend them on high speed for 1 min. .
2. Once the time is up, serve it right away and enjoy.

Detox Pear Cucumber Smoothie
(ready in about 2 minutes | Servings 2)

Ingredients:

- ½ pear, chopped
- ¼ cup of cilantro, chopped
- ½ avocado,
- ½ cucumber, chopped
- ¼ lemon, sliced
- ¾ inch of fresh ginger, sliced
- ¾ cup of coconut water
- ¼ cup of protein powder
- 1 ½ cups of kale
- 2 cups of water

Directions:

1. Combine all the ingredients in your Ninja Blender and blend them on high speed for 45 sec.

2. Once the time is up, serve it right away and enjoy.

Iron Booster Beet Apple Smoothie
(ready in about 2 minutes | Servings 2)

Ingredients:

- 1 ½ lemon, peeled and sliced
- 2 cups of kale leaves
- 1/3 cup of parsley
- 16 ounces of purified water
- 2 tablespoons of chia seeds
- 1 medium sized beet, peeled and sliced
- 2 apples, sliced

Directions:

1. Combine all the ingredients in your Ninja Blender and blend them on high speed until they become smooth.
2. Serve your smoothie right away and enjoy.

Antioxidant Rich Minty Berries Apple Smoothie

(ready in about 2 minutes | Servings 2)

Ingredients:

- 10 leaves of mint
- 1 apple, cored and sliced
- 20 fluid ounces of purified water
- 5 romaine lettuce leaves
- ½ cup of mixed berries

Directions:

1. Combine all the ingredients in your Ninja Blender and blend them on high speed for 45 sec.
2. Once the time is up, serve it right away and enjoy.

Cleansing Bluish Ginger Smoothie
(ready in about 2 minutes | Servings 2)

Ingredients:

- 2 bananas, frozen
- ½ cup of ginger juice
- 2 ½ cups of soy sauce
- 4 ice cubes
- ½ cup of blue berries

Directions:

1. Combine all the ingredients in your Ninja Blender and blend them on high speed for 45 sec.
2. Once the time is up, serve it right away and enjoy.

Detox Lemon Smoothie
(ready in about 2 minutes | Servings 2)

Ingredients:

- 3 ounces of protein powder
- ¼ cucumber, sliced
- 1 cup of kale leaves
- ½ avocado
- 3 tablespoons of cilantro leaves
- ½ ounces of fresh ginger, sliced
- ¼ lemon, sliced

Directions:

1. Combine all the ingredients in your Ninja Blender and blend them on high speed for 45 sec.
2. Once the time is up, serve it right away and enjoy.

Alkalizing Cranberry Smoothie
(ready in about 2 minutes | Servings 2)

Ingredients:

- 1 celery stalk, sliced
- 1 ½ apple, cored and chopped
- 1 cucumber, sliced
- ¾ cup of cranberries
- 2 cups of purified water
- 1 ½ pear, sliced
- ½ cup of spinach

Directions:

1. Combine all the ingredients in your Ninja Blender and blend them on high speed for 1 min.
2. Once the time is up, serve it right away and enjoy.

Radiant Skin Cherry Berry Smoothie
(ready in about 2 minutes | Servings 2)

Ingredients:

- 1 cup of raspberries, frozen
- 1 cup of almond milk
- 1 ½ tablespoon of fresh ginger, sliced
- 2 ½ tablespoons of honey
- 2/3 cup of cherries, frozen
- 1 tablespoon of lemon juice
- 2 teaspoons of flax seeds

Directions:

1. Combine all the ingredients in your Ninja Blender and blend them on high speed for 45 sec.

2. Once the time is up, serve it right away and enjoy.

Anti-Aging Bomb Berries Summit
(ready in about 2 minutes | Servings 2)

Ingredients:

- 1 ½ cup of coconut milk
- ¼ cup of goji berries
- ¾ cup of raspberries
- 5 dates, pitted
- 2 cups of purified water
- ¾ cup of blackberries
- 2 tablespoons of flax seeds
- 1 ½ cups of blueberries

Directions:

1. Combine all the ingredients in your Ninja Blender and blend them on high speed for 1 min.
2. Once the time is up, serve it right away and enjoy.

Healthy Heart Pear Avocado Smoothie
(ready in about 2 minutes | Servings 2)

Ingredients:

- 1 pear, sliced
- 1 ½ cups of spinach
- 1 /2 cup of protein powder
- 2 ½ cups of water
- ½ cup of coconut water
- 1 tablespoon of chia seeds
- ½ avocado
- 2 cups of almond milk

Directions:

1. Combine all the ingredients in your Ninja Blender and blend them on high speed for 45 sec.
2. Once the time is up, serve it right away and enjoy.

Super Models Secret Creamy Goji Berries Smoothie

(ready in about 2 minutes | Servings 2)

Ingredients:

- ½ cup of strawberries
- ½ cup of goji berries
- 4 ice cubes
- 2 ½ cups of coconut water
- 2 bananas

Directions:

1. Combine all the ingredients in your Ninja Blender and blend them on high speed for 1 min.
2. Once the time is up, serve it right away and enjoy.

Green Monster Jicama Smoothie
(ready in about 2 minutes | Servings 2)

Ingredients:

- 1 cup of jicama
- 10 romaine leaves
- 3 pitted dates
- 2 ½ cup of water
- ½ cup of protein powder
- ½ cup of cilantro, finely chopped
- 1 cucumber, sliced
- 1 avocado
- 1 lime
- 1 apple

Directions:
1. Combine all the ingredients in your Ninja Blender and blend them on high speed for 1 min.
2. Once the time is up, serve it right away and enjoy.

Alkalizing Orange Smoothie
(ready in about 2 minutes | Servings 2)

Ingredients:

- ¼ cup of parsley leaves, chopped
- 1 ½ cups of mango, diced
- 1 ½ cups of kale leaves, chopped
- 1 ½ cups of orange juice
- 1 ½ cups of celery stems, chopped

Directions:

1. Combine all the ingredients in your Ninja Blender and blend them on high speed for 45 sec.
2. Once the time is up, serve it right away and enjoy.

Healthy Liver Limy Coconut Smoothie
(ready in about 2 minutes | Servings 2)

Ingredients:

- 1 cup of coconut water
- 2 tablespoons of coconut oil
- ¾ cup of parsley leaves
- 1 cucumber
- 2 cups of purified water
- 2 apples, sliced
- 1 ½ limes, sliced
- 3 tablespoons of mint leaves

Directions:

1. Combine all the ingredients in your Ninja Blender and blend them on high speed for 1 min.
2. Once the time is up, serve it right away and enjoy.

Clean Gut Spicy Tomato Smoothie
(ready in about 2 minutes | Servings 2)

Ingredients:

- 3 celery stalks, sliced
- 2 bell red peppers, seeded sliced
- 3 tomatoes, chopped
- ½ cup of water cress
- 1 red jalapeno, seeded and sliced
- 1 cup of spinach
- 3 cloves of garlic, peeled
- 5 carrots, chopped

Directions:

1. Combine all the ingredients in your Ninja Blender and blend them on high speed for 45 sec.
2. Once the time is up, serve it right away and enjoy.

Superfood Creamy Spirulina Smoothie
(ready in about 2 minutes | Servings 2)

Ingredients:

- 2 cups of water
- ½ cup of protein powder
- 1 cup of blueberries
- 1 tablespoon of Spirulina powder
- 1 cup of almond milk
- 1 banana
- ½ avocado

Directions:

1. Combine all the ingredients in your Ninja Blender and blend them on high speed for 45 sec.
2. Once the time is up, serve it right away and enjoy.

Cleansing Mango Kale Smoothie
(ready in about 2 minutes | Servings 2)

Ingredients:

- 1 cup of orange juice
- 1 cup of kale leaves
- ¼ cup of parsley leaves
- 1 stalk of celery, chopped
- ½ cup of mango chunks

Directions:

1. Combine all the ingredients in your Ninja Blender and blend them on high speed for 45 sec.
2. Once the time is up, serve it right away and enjoy.

Glowing Skin Summery Strawberry Lemon Smoothie

(ready in about 2 minutes | Servings 2)

Ingredients:
- 3 ½ cups of almond milk
- 1 ½ banana, frozen
- 1 orange, sliced
- 2 cups of spinach
- 1 ½ tablespoons of lemon zest
- 2 ½ cups of strawberries

Directions:

1. Combine all the ingredients in your Ninja Blender and blend them on high speed for 45 sec.
2. Once the time is up, serve it right away and enjoy.

Fat Burner Lemony Apple Smoothie
(ready in about 2 minutes | Servings 2)

Ingredients:

- 16 ounces of purified water
- 2 teaspoon of barely grass powder
- 2 apples, sliced
- 1 cucumber, chopped
- 1 ½ lemons, seedless and sliced
- ½ cup of mango chunks
- 5 leaves of red lettuce

Directions:

1. Combine all the ingredients in your Ninja Blender and blend them on high speed for 1 min.
2. Once the time is up, serve it right away and enjoy.

Fight Cholesterol Lime Almond Smoothie
(ready in about 2 minutes | Servings 2)

Ingredients:

- 1 cup of almond milk
- 1 banana, frozen
- 1 ½ cup of spinach
- 5 ice cubes
- 2 dates, pitted
- ½ cup of lime juice
- 2 tablespoons of almond butter

Directions:

1. Combine all the ingredients in your Ninja Blender and blend them on high speed for 45 sec.
2. Once the time is up, serve it right away and enjoy.

Kid-Friendly Tropical Avocado Smoothie
(ready in about 2 minutes | Servings 2)

Ingredients:

- 1 tablespoon of chia seeds
- 1 cup of ice cubes
- ½ cup of spring water
- 2 tablespoon of honey
- ½ banana, frozen
- 1/3 cup of lime juice
- ½ mango
- ½ avocado

Directions:

1. Combine all the ingredients in your Ninja Blender and blend them on high speed for 45 sec.
2. Once the time is up, serve it right away and enjoy.

Clear Skin Pear Summer Smoothie
(ready in about 2 minutes | Servings 2)

Ingredients:

- ½ cup of apple juice
- ½ pear
- 1 apple, cored and sliced
- 1 stalk of celery, chopped
- 1 cup of kale
- 1 tablespoon of fresh ginger, sliced
- 1 cup of ice cubes

Directions:

1. Combine all the ingredients in your Ninja Blender and blend them on high speed for 45 sec.
2. Once the time is up, serve it right away and enjoy.

Blood Pressure Cucumber Beet Smoothie
(ready in about 2 minutes | Servings 2)

Ingredients:

- ½ beet, sliced
- 1 carrot
- ½ cup of spring water
- 1 celery stalk, chopped
- ½ cucumber, chopped
- 1 tablespoon of ginger, sliced
- 1 cup of ice cubes

Directions:

1. Combine all the ingredients in your Ninja Blender and blend them on high speed for 45 sec.
2. Once the time is up, serve it right away and enjoy.

Red Velvet Veggies Smoothie
(ready in about 2 minutes | Servings 2)

Ingredients:

- ½ red bell pepper, chopped
- 1 celery stalk, chopped
- 1 cup of ice cubes
- 1 cup of kale
- 1 tomato
- 2 cloves of garlic
- 1 carrot

Directions:

1. Combine all the ingredients in your Ninja Blender and blend them on high speed for 45 sec.
2. Once the time is up, serve it right away and enjoy.

Forever Young Blue Royal Smoothie
(ready in about 2 minutes | Servings 2)

Ingredients:

- 1 cup of coconut water
- ½ avocado
- ¾ cup of blueberries
- ½ banana
- 1 cup of kale
- ½ cucumber

Directions:

1. Combine all the ingredients in your Ninja Blender and blend them on high speed for 45 sec.
2. Once the time is up, serve it right away and enjoy.

Weight Loss Almond Berry Smoothie
(ready in about 2 minutes | Servings 2)

Ingredients:

- ½ cup of blueberries
- 1 cup of almond milk
- ½ cup of ice cubes
- 1 cup of honeydew melon
- ½ cup of green grapes, seedless
- 1 apple, sliced
- 1 cup of kale
- 1 kiwi

Directions:

1. Combine all the ingredients in your Ninja Blender and blend them on high speed for 45 sec.
2. Once the time is up, serve it right away and enjoy.

Perfect Morning Green Spring Smoothie
(ready in about 2 minutes | Servings 2)

Ingredients:

- ¼ cup of spring water
- 1 apple, sliced
- 1 cup of ice cubes
- 1 stalk of celery, chopped
- 1 cup of kale
- 1/3 cucumber, sliced
- 1 tablespoon of lemon juice

Directions:

1. Combine all the ingredients in your Ninja Blender and blend them on high speed for 45 sec.
2. Once the time is up, serve it right away and enjoy.

Healthy Dessert Vanilla Caramel
(ready in about 2 minutes | Servings 2)

Ingredients:

- 1 cup of vanilla yogurt, low fat
- 1 tablespoon of cinnamon
- ¼ cup of caramel sauce
- 6 ice cubes
- 2 cups of apple juice
- 2 tablespoons of sweetener

Directions:

1. Combine all the ingredients in your Ninja Blender and blend them on high speed for 45 sec.
2. Once the time is up, serve it right away and enjoy.

No Constipation Cheesy Vanilla Tart
(ready in about 2 minutes | Servings 2)

Ingredients:

- 1 ½ banana
- 2 cups of vanilla almond milk
- ¼ cup of low fat cream cheese
- ½ teaspoon of cinnamon
- 1 cup of low fat vanilla yogurt
- ½ cup of low fat cottage cheese

Directions:

1. Combine all the ingredients in your Ninja Blender and blend them on high speed for 45 sec.
2. Once the time is up, serve it right away and enjoy.

Huge Muscle Protein Berry Smoothie
(ready in about 2 minutes | Servings 2)

Ingredients:

- 1 cup of low fat milk
- 1 cup of mixed berries, frozen
- 2 cups of orange juice
- ¼ cup of protein powder
- 2 tablespoons of chia seeds
- 1 ½ carrot

Directions:

1. Combine all the ingredients in your Ninja Blender and blend them on high speed for 45 sec.
2. Once the time is up, serve it right away and enjoy.

Post Workout Creamy Honey Tofu
(ready in about 2 minutes | Servings 2)

Ingredients:

- ¼ cup of honey
- 3 cups of mixed berries, frozen
- 2 cups of pomegranate juice
- 2 cups of silken tofu

Directions:

1. Combine all the ingredients in your Ninja Blender and blend them on high speed for 45 sec.
2. Once the time is up, serve it right away and enjoy.

Energy Booster Banana Coffee
(ready in about 2 minutes | Servings 2)

Ingredients:

- ½ cup of low fat milk
- ½ cup of dry oats
- 2 cups of brewed coffee
- 1 ½ bananas
- ½ cup of protein powder
- 2 tablespoons of sweetener

Directions:

1. Combine all the ingredients in your Ninja Blender and blend them on high speed for 45 sec.
2. Once the time is up, serve it right away and enjoy.

Glowing Green Kale Smoothie
(ready in about 2 minutes | Servings 2)

Ingredients:

- 1 cup of kale
- 1/3 cup of cilantro, chopped
- ½ lemon, sliced
- 1 ½ cup of spring water
- 1 wedge of lime
- 2 tablespoons of sweetener

Directions:

1. Combine all the ingredients in your Ninja Blender and blend them on high speed for 1 min.
2. Once the time is up, serve it right away and enjoy.

Your Free Gift

I wanted to show my appreciation that you support my work so I've put together a free gift for you.

Slowcooker Essentials Cookbook
http://thezenfactory.com/nutri_ninja_pro_free_book/

Just visit the link above to download it now.

I know you will love this gift.

Thanks!

Conclusion

Thank you again for downloading this book! I really do hope you found the recipes as tasty and mouth watering as I did.

☐ **Copyright by Daniel Hinkle All rights reserved.**

This document is geared towards providing exact and reliable information in regards to the topic and issue covered. The publication is sold with the idea that the publisher is not required to render accounting, officially permitted, or otherwise, qualified services. If advice is necessary, legal or professional, a practiced individual in the profession should be ordered.

- From a Declaration of Principles which was accepted and approved equally by a Committee of the American Bar Association and a Committee of Publishers and Associations.

In no way is it legal to reproduce, duplicate, or transmit any part of this document in either electronic means or in printed format. Recording of this publication is strictly prohibited and any storage of this document is not allowed unless with written permission from the publisher. All rights reserved.

The information provided herein is stated to be truthful and consistent, in that any liability, in terms of inattention or otherwise, by any usage or abuse of any policies, processes, or directions contained within is the solitary and utter responsibility of the recipient reader. Under no circumstances will any legal responsibility or blame be held against the publisher for any reparation, damages, or monetary loss due to the information herein, either directly or indirectly.
Respective authors own all copyrights not held by the publisher.

The information herein is offered for informational purposes solely, and is universal as so. The presentation of the information is without contract or any type of guarantee assurance.

The trademarks that are used are without any consent, and the publication of the trademark is without permission or backing by the trademark owner. All trademarks and brands within this book are for clarifying purposes only and are the owned by the owners themselves, not affiliated with this document.